LOVE, ADDICTION, AND EVERYTHING BETWEEN THE LINES

PHILLIP "LEGAND" JAMES

authorHOUSE

AuthorHouse™
1663 Liberty Drive
Bloomington, IN 47403
www.authorhouse.com
Phone: 833-262-8899

Published by AuthorHouse 11/30/2020

ISBN: 978-1-6655-0944-2 (sc)
ISBN: 978-1-6655-0943-5 (e)

Print information available on the last page.

This book is printed on acid-free paper.

ACKNOWLEDGEMENT

Nothing is possible without shared experiences with others. That being said thank you to everyone I shared a moment, an experience or a sequence of events with. Every single one of you help me get here no matter how large or small your part is in my miniscule movie entitled my life.

You always think you have the time to give those in your life their flowers until you don't. But I won't waste this opportunity to thank you Big Homie(Frank Carter). You always appreciated my penmanship for what it is and would always take a moment to remind me I have something worth sharing. Thank you for being a good man and inspiration. Rest in Paradise my G

Special thanks to my brother from another mother, my best friend and alter ego. Curtis Spencer A.k.a "Doja the Beat Connoisseur". You never missed a moment to appreciate my talent and push me to share that talent with the world. Without you putting the steering wheel in my back I wouldn't have seen this through. You will always be remembered and loved. Rest in Paradise my G.

Last but always first in my life, Thank you Sharon Williams my mother, mentor and life coach. You did everything you could to save me from myself and I still almost threw it all away. Thank you for never giving up on me and always being there. Every line I write is to make your purchase of my first laptop worth it. Love you.

LUST OR IS IT LOVE

I only get to imagine

That this is real

Held captive in a rem state

Where cupids design for us is fulfilled

Because in our current reality

That "this" doesn't exist

And the possibility that this lust

Could become love has made me ill.

As my emotions balance reality and truth

I can only allow my imagination to run ramped

Intertwined in thoughts of you- and I will

Imagine that your touch will allow me

To remove emotional doubts

Believing in the foundation of forever

As our relationship builds.

If the bliss in "this" existed

In the present tense and your adoration

Was something I could feel

Your touch would become the springs

I used to heal passionate wounds

Allowing my imagination to rebuild

My thoughts of love surrounding you

But I remain under the clutch

Of the what ifs.

In a rocking chair I sit

Eyes wide shut sense engaged

Seeing our future clear

Lost in the euphoric acceptance

Of this rem state of distrust.

If lust can become love

If honesty still leads to distrust

Could lust ever turn into love?

If love is a form of lust

Then this form of us is natural

And could be the formula

That turns lust into love.

The other night I was being polite

I really wanted to pull you close

And get lost in your eyes

Lose ourselves in the night

Anchored by an experience we can

Cherish for the rest of our lives

But the gentleman in me

Told me to play the nice guy.

But if I was ever presented

A second chance I'd advance

Like we've never meet

Willing to do any and everything you like

Just give me a sign.

PASSION

"I WON'T BE"

Hindered by your expectations of passion

Of what could be, should be

Or what has been those

Are just empty promise and experiences

That deserve to be past tense

And this is PASSION!

Passion that I wish to share

With you, so what ifs become

Nonfactors If the sum of

Two parts Is us sharing a mood

In the same room.

I spark a L and look forward

To the sun looking in your eyes

I inhale again and look deeper

Inside to uncover what makes you shine

Under the reflection of the moon.

I am willing to do

Whatever to see how your body moves

Which makes me not bothered

By other suitors in suits

With no suitable conversational que to use

Expressing their admiration and cool

Because I am different.

I know you hear

These guys say a lot

But I am the only one who speaks

And piques your interest

With new information on what your

Interested in to encourage you to listen.

Please.

These are not just pleasantries

When I say good morning

I want you to notice

That this passion is everything.

AMOROUS JUSTICE

If it's just us

For the rest of our lives

That is justice

-N- if it's just tonight

I want to see forever in your eyes

As complete devotion

Is reflected from mine

I want to trust us.

A slow pace can manipulate

Our perspective of time

Roles played and inebriated

Photoshoots as time flies

Positions change and moments intensifies

Each time we switch the high

Lines following paper planes

Become a chem trail

When sensuality is combined.

So...........

Don't rush imagination or this groove

You know the vibes, soulful

I am still mesmerized

By your aura and how you move

Your timeless

I am yours, do what you want to

I am your property to use

Just try it.

In this moment, every fantasy fulfilled

Is an experienced shared

I promise to keep it private

I am eager to show and prove

That your safe here.

I want to hold you

But I will not hold you

I want to- Do you justice.

RANDOM #5

I will be the first to say, I cannot fight

But I will fight you niggas

Let this left offset the right

And properly dress the eyes

Of you niggas

I'm fishing with negativity

For positive attention

Manipulating the energy

And supplying the tools for their addiction

Change literally staring them

In the face but their claims

Of disbelief caused them to miss it.

The truth in the devil eyes

Can be found in the faith of a Christian

It's all make believe until you need

Belief to make life worth living

Though with no direction your just tracing

The steps of mismanaged spirits.

I swear I cannot fight

But I put these fist up

After I raise one fist in remembrance

Of the struggle that defines us.

From that stance is nothing but

Black eyes and missing teeth

For punch drunk punks that believe

They can't get punched – I swear I can't fight.

THE SAME ENERGY

Can we, keep that same energy

We had when

Anticipation and imagination

Catered to our levels of intimacy

That same energy

That found passion in curiosity

Excitement in the wonder

Of a touch in hopes of another.

That energy that allowed

Lust to carry us further

Into each other, what we share

Is the foundation of chemistry

But still my aura approaches you like

You one fine muthafucka….

That's the energy I want us to keep.

That I'm looking at you

Looking at me, watching your lips

You know you are about to be

Late to work and your body screams

That will be time well spent.

The silence that accompanies

That thought makes the situation more intense

Intensely I grab onto the energy

Between us, each position becomes

A lasting image in the sheets

Of the energy that adds excitement – TO OUR LOVE!

THE STARS LIED

I looked to the sky for guidance

And the stars lied to me

Showing me possibilities as a future reality

The irony, my admiration for emotional prosperity

Is hiding in smokey fields of green.

The envy in it, is my personal enemy.

Though those scenes

Where never meant to be seen

I ask, am I being taunted

By an omniscient being?

In the stars I see two faces

With a path to two lives

Both capable of providing me

The comfort of a King.

But when I step down- from the clouds

Relaxing in my High

Three becomes a crowd and magnetically

The attraction has my internal compass

Lost in the forest of my heart strings.

Should I head North and grow

With a similar spirit or reconvene down south

With energy with similar interest

The alchemy of true love

Validates hopeful intuition.

I look to the stars for guidance

And realize if I continue to look up

I will eventually look past us

So, I stay focused on the path

That guides our love.

LOVE IS NOT A SITCOM- ACT 1
(THE FIGHT IN THE BEDROOM)

When love changes

That does not mean

It can't be better

When we rarely see love

In each other's faces

Complacency becomes the only

Reason we stay together.

But you say "If it's love"

Why change now when we have forever

But tomorrow isn't promised

So, I am rushing towards change

To make our todays better.

Whenever, Wherever, Whatever

Has changed to

I have never, you have never,

Nigga fuck you, Bitch whatever

You want it like it was

I'm like I seen that movie once

And walked out before the credits.

I keep telling you

"I'm giving you all my love"

You keep talking about the past

But your actions remain speechless in the present

If we do not live, how can we make love last?

LOVE IS NOT A SITCOM— ACT 2
(RESOLUTION AT THE FRONT DOOR)

You're my Francine Smith

Rose Garden and All

And I'm your Stan

Stubborn with flaws but

You act like you don't know

I am devoted to your flag.

Which means any vested interest

I have in what makes her interesting

Is purely plutonic, her presence could never

Threaten what we have – emotionally

Would my house be a home

If I was not completely honest?

How could I ever put a courtier

In the position of my Queen?

That is the help, but reality

Has never been the basis of belief.

Though even if you choose to leave

You will remain a Queen to me

In the arms of another King

Or out on your own

I love you enough to honor

The truth you know.

That is what I wanted to say

Before the door closed.

GOOD TIMES- IT'S A VIBE

Good Times

Good weed, Jazz beats, it's a vibe

The mood is set

For you to undress

In due time.

Good Times

Intriguing conversation and witty lines

Disguise my freaky motives

Behind gentle eyes.

It's a Vibe

A good high and a few lines

Enhance the experiences we share

As we unwind

Good Times I challenge you intellectually

You gladly accept and return in kind.

It's a Vibe

I see your aura as we sit

Silently over a glass of wine

I get to know you more

As your body language says

Everything you are trying to hide.

Good Times

I don't want to say

Goodbye, Good Evening, nor Good Night.

Because…

Tonight, I've gotten closer to you

And got lost in the vibes

This moment…

The sax blowing more weed rolling

We've dimmed the lights.

Anticipation my hearts racing

I'm breathing different

What happens next can be

Summed up in a simple sentence

We had a good time.

I.T.O.U
(I THINK OF YOU)

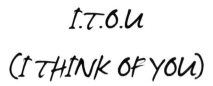

Lost in the thought of you

As smoke fills my lungs

Then fills the room with silhouettes

That patterns its movements

Around how your body moves

More smoke More smoke – Short Stroke Long Stroke

In my memories you taste like passion fruit.

OMG I.T.O.U - When traces of your fragrance

Fills the room and your previous phrases

Become tattooed statements on my

Emotional sleeve that I look at

To elevate my mood.

I Think of You

And become enamored by our chemistry

An exploration of our Intellect

Has led to a higher level of intimacy

The time elapse bares the proof.

Baby you go the juice and you got me open

I.T.O.U defines the moment

When fantasies become timeless

And I get lost in the moment

That star my P.Y.T. in her birthday suit

The blunt got my attention I hit it

Then I think of you.

YOUR DEVOTED ZEALOT

I would let you seduce me

Take advantage of my innocents and use me

I will do the things I said I'll

Never do if it pleases you immensely.

I surrender to your aura

Commit to your desires

You have become the tree

That gives my life meaning

And takes me higher – do what thy wilt.

I am your passionate follower

Baptized in your water

You give me a reason to feel

An even better reason to kneel

You are my Queen.

Do what you want with me

I am your subject to control

Taxed by your passion

Regulated by your seduction

I don't get off until you say so

The restraints temper the pain

And provides a safe space

For the pleasure to ride a high note.

I am a slave to your wants

A victim of your sensuality

So please violate my erotic civilities

As you are casually up the intensity

The leash keeps me tamed

The paddle stings, the ropes burn

But I love the pleasure it brings

I am yours.

OUR LAST CONVERSATION

I replay our last conversation

And I hang on to every word

Intimate and intelligent language

Had me ready to take

The intellectual property of a verb

And take action though I listened and waited.

The mental space of euphoria

You created with your

Perspective of the moment love happens

Provided a safe space

For my emotions to flourish

In the elements of passion.

Each syllable in every phrase

Was captivating and enchanting

I swear your aura is a reflection

Of true magic so…. Cast away!

Put me under your spell I am a willing participant

In any and every experience made

Bewitched by your radiant beauty

I am affected by everything

You have said and have to say

Your essence is everything understood

That can not be explained

Your words are the literature

That gives purpose to my day- Our last conversation.

FOREVER TODAY

A day like today

Is made for us

To sit in our grays

Listening to the rain and

The joyous hymns of Mary Jane

Start a new series on Netflix

And chill in each other's shade.

If a day

Was ever meant to be perfect

Then a day like today

Deserves that verbiage

Because even though our

Birthdays don't coincide with this date

Those suits fit like we earned it.

Your presence adds value to my day

Your essence is

The proverbial dollar from fifteen cents

That has given me new life

While taking my breath away.

So naturally your gifts

Are an Ode to Classical Art

The meaning is in the experience

And the experience changes you

In such positive ways.

But I swear if I could

Manipulate time and extend

Every moment In this day

When I saw a reflection of

Love in your eyes.

Then the forever in love

Can be defined

In the memory of your embrace

In which I currently reside.

I am just saying

"I'll make time move slow"

Like the sands in God Eye

Or like

That bead of water

Dripping down your thigh

I am so into you.

RANDOM # 6

Ancient Aliens and Bomb Weed

Political ideals and a tight booty Queen

White Supremacist and white lines

That propel my cool as skis

To the polar opposites that define

My American Dream.

Everything is what it seems

When there is nothing to gain

The ol will stay the same

When there is a profit to be made

So there no house for a hoe

And that will never change.

The same could be said

For my pen game

That will remain too dope

6:66 ahead of the next frame

As I excel in my old age

Blowing pre-rollled.

In the next frame

Ancient Aliens provide foresight

Into the action of my enemies

The bomb ass weed

Helps me kill them all

From a position of power and peace.

Now with a mask on

They all kneel to the King.

EYES WIDE SHUT
OR
AFTER THE RED PILL

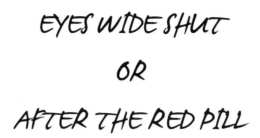

With my eyes closed

I see you clearer

Then I have before

As sensuality radiates from your aura

Guiding me to the source.

I am traveling through closed doors

To save the love I've

Always felt but have never known

The oracle gave purpose to your adoration

So, I blindly swallow

The colored pill of your choice

Just to save it.

With my hands tied I've felt passion

In curves I believed to be lost

Like cupids' arrow in the Matrix

As I watch you slide of your red dress

I lose myself in anticipation.

The six paces you take to my bed

Appear in slow motion

And in that moment

I experienced six levels of passion

And discovered six ways to explore

Your naked forest.

My gorgeous seductress

A goddess but so devilish

I am a slave to your mental seduction

In awe of your verbal powers.

You make me feel like

I've never known lust, been touched

Or experienced love until you

Found me lost and your time

Gave meaning to the hour.

With my eyes wide shut

My nose is wide open lead by

The eternal fragrance of love

Though the restraints keep me motionless

Your silhouette dances around my senses

Such an exhilarating experience

The constant flow of beautiful imagery

Is endless in the darkest space

Like the depths of our oceans.

With your hands in motion

I yearn for you to keep going

Your lips everywhere I want them

Your tongue is telling my favorite story

And I want you to keep going

The attention you give me is special

And I know it

I keep my eyes wide shut as you keep going.

ROLEPLAY

You put that outfit on

And change for me

My shy girl turned femme fatal

Showcasing her curves radiating sensual energy

Letting me know she is ready now

The way you display your strength

In your new clothes

Pinning me to the floor

Has me digging your style

As I surrender as the villain

In anticipation of more

My Black Widow tangle me

In your web in the shade

As we explore fifty ways

For you to express your freak

Tie me up and let me

Marvel at your beauty as you keep

Your passionate intentions a secret

Avenging the sheets destroyed

By the last position

And then…

You put that outfit on

And change for me

Turning into my Thmyescrian Queen

My wonder woman

Demanding what she wants

Taking what she needs

With appropriate gusto

Retrain me with your lasso

Which in this moment is

As precious as gold

Then force me to revel my most

Intimate desires leaving me

Emotionally exposed

As you lose yourself in this role

I call you my super woman

In return you show me

How well you can perform

With that outfit on

Your no longer my shy girl

As you place my face where no man

Can continue to call home

And then…

You put that outfit on

And change for me.

IMPASSIONED MOMENT

When we share a moment like this
I wish we could exist
Amongst the stairs and
In that moment love lifespan
Would span ten lifetimes
To ensure passion and admiration
Exudes from where we are
Because together- we shine!

When we have moments like that
On a night like this
I experience each scenario like
It's the first time
We shared an experience
With a like mind.

Though likewise each scene
Is felt through a prism of a
Reoccurring past life
So, it's safe to say my love
For you has traveled through time
On a repetitive loop.

I no longer look to answer
The question to life pondering truth
Because its evident that the "why"
Is you, I have the evidence!

It has been preordained in destiny name

No wait I will just say

When you find a mountain to climb

You don't look for a rock to move

Your my foundation

The soil that bares my futures fruit.

The statement

Of love the defies all time

Your energy is the sands that

Give me reason to be alive

My life, my love, my energy

Belongs to nobody but you.

So, in a moment like this

I look for the North Star

To guide me to Oshun

Then humbly request to cheat death

Under the stars

To bring beauty to the moon

As a gift of my everlasting devotion

To you…

NO END TO BELIEF

The truth is more of a belief

And less of fact

Though my truth is everything

I believe and that's a

Matter of Fact.

My beliefs become the truth

I used to justify my nefarious acts

The means are just that

When there isn't an end attached

Which just means

My addiction has a permanent

Place in my Fannie Pack.

Opinions feel good and sound

Like the truth so it is

The truth makes you react

Emotionally so its sincerity

Is easily dismissed and we

Become the propaganda of

Fake News as the truth spins

In a web of deceit.

The guilty can become the innocent

For an appropriate fee

The innocent can remain guilty

When they were never intended

To be free

Everything was never what it was

And exactly how it seems

I've been woke so long

The shadows are starting to speak.

In a religious tone

Offering me the power of belief

Now the truth is an artform

Taught to those looking

'To follow her lead.

PENNING PURPOSE

I write

Emotions from emotionless pictures

Deceptive images

From the perspective of a sinner

On top of a righteous pedestal

Held up by promiscuous women.

While I blow dro and lose myself

In the rolled dollars that

Carry me to my ambitions

Over falling rose petals.

I developed this talent

In my penmanship

The moment I discovered

Religion- peeped the manuscript

Then turned it into a lifetime

Of fly sentences find a reason

That's what I write for.

For those left outdoors

Mislead and gifted for my toxic individuals

With a swisher rolled and coce

For the bitches

Dreds with a book to give

And Charlatans with a mouth full

With no real social interest

I write to maintain, what real and authentic.

INDIGENOUS CRAYOLA

They refuse to see

The complexity and beauty

In my dark skin

So how can they presume

To understand my mentality

And social intent.

When the shallow waters

On the surface appear

To dark and deep

For a comfortable swim towards

Like minded intelligence.

To whom does that make sense?

Oh yeah the ignorant

So, I pay no mind to that

As I entertain myself with

Reflective thoughts of ignorance.

I'm dehydrated and aggy

Losing patients with my sanity

Line after line of death and destruction

I'm the embodiment of a successful

Rap scheme and with two
Finger guns used figuratively
I've identified popular influence
And what's beef.

Rightfully addressed as your highness
As I sit on a pedestal of honesty
With a leaf proclaiming only God
Has seen more consecutive days
As high as me.

I've seen the truth you seek
And it's a lie
Is it ironic the sons and daughters
Of the most high
Willingly lose themselves in the light
Trying to shine.

While I enter the dragon lair
To find the glow
Shonuff ready to die for mine
Because you can't win the fight
Fighting from the outside.

FRONT POARCH CONVERSATION

I've heard

Those searching

For fulfillment through ignorance

All say

"I'm doing this the for the culture"

"Representing like a real nigga supposed ta"

STOP IT LIAR.

Now that same energy

Is in the soil

We used to grow our seeds

Hence how a destructive perception

Deceives and repeats.

You first must understand

The power of choice

Before you can comprehend

The power of belief

And upon that realization

The power of words

Becomes a tangible being

You can manipulate to gain

Power over minds and receive

All of life luxuries.

Now that is deep

Nah them is shallow waters

That resemble the depths

Of the Hennessey you use

To drown your problems.

Now that's a pill

They do not want to sallow

To feel like Phil

But I'm just here to make you think.

If I dared to dream

A dreamer dream

In hopes that faith

Will protect me from adversity

Then like them

I would believe the credit

For my life disappointments

Belong to someone other than me.

But I'm the man

Who dream formulate foresight

Into the nuances

That drive mice and men

THE DEVIL WHISPERS CONFIDENCE IN TRUTH

Kill, Kill, Kill

Whispers from my pen

On weed coce and pills

So that's all I hear

In this prism where only

White noise carries a pitch.

A glass of Red Rum

Disguises the murderous intent

Kill at will cause I'm Ill for real

Damn those whispers again

If the ignorant cease to exist

Would the moderately intelligent

Continue to excel in common sense?

The will to execute

For the better good

Brings purpose to my sentences

And will balance the weight

Of a feather when I am

Sentenced by him.

Kill, Kill, Kill

The Black Queen, Families and the

Ideology of the Black Fist

Prosperity through genocide

Is the American Dream

That defines our independence.

Mary Jane, Boy George, and Nurse Jackie

Are my only friends

So it's safe to say

I'm focused spiritually manipulating

The energies we use to live.

Fuck how you feel

Exceeding my potential using steel

To sharpen steel

Tell me who is real

Aww man there goes another one

Gone missing again.

Whispers from the devil tongue

Validates the wisdom in a penny

The cost of the precious gift

Is understanding your value

In the present she whispers to me.

Whispers and whispers to me

Death is best understood by those

Who chose to live life to the fullest.

In my ride a mistress and a side chick

To pass the time

Destiny and fate introduce me

To the luxurious pains in life

With dreamy eyes and without

Guilt I obey the whispers

Leaving my mark on mankind.

RANDOM PT. 4 (FOR MY BROTHER)

The synonyms for the unintelligent

Have become positive pleasantries

While elegant speech is condemned

As a product of the other side.

We foolishly cross those lines

And justify spending our money

On fashion that was designed

Without us in mind and

To mock our pain and pride.

All because

We chose not to think for ourselves

And those we idolized

Convinced us to believe

We must sever our cultural ties

If we want to see our dreams

Of financial prosperity materialize.

Though all is fair and should be

Expected in the pursuit of wealth

So, it's no surprise

The dollar sign attached to

Black lives fluctuate like a gas price.

You only get one life

But the sequel is endured

By the love ones you leave behind.

Please think for yourself.

POPULAR QUALITY VS QUALITY JEWELS

Just because it's popular

Does not make it quality

Tommy wasn't designed to cover black skin

Crystal wasn't meant to accompany

The promiscuous interest of black men

The lesson in this is

Everything cost even the underline intent.

Similarly

A voluptuous stripper

Can tell you her real name

Though a hoe by a different name

Is still a hoe

If there was a profit made

To a Dick, with a

Head full of honesty.

Ignorant sensibilities and a reference to Malcom

Does not make you Nas like

If the message is distorting the energy

And helping the darkness subsume the light

Now if you're an emcee

You can say Nigga if the beat is nice

But if a white boy catches the beats

For saying nigga a black man has

To question if his actions are justified

Weird Shit…

But we stay focused on the wrong fight

Our morals our lost in the throws

Of a good time

Those selling us the American Dream

Have over indulged in perversion

Now perverse behavior is normalized.

The complexity of common sense

Is daunting to popular intellect

Mental health is a tool

The uninvolved use for likes.

So, when we talk about the quality

Of life imitating art

It isn't hard to see

In a sea of mediocrity

The best parts

OF the art has died.

They swear it is quality

But can't tell you why

Though everyone is on the bridge

Attempting to fly

Just to be

Where the popular populace resides.

LISTEN WHEN WISDOM IS FREE

Everything I learned due

To an emotional betrayal

Was once an experience shared

I dismissed as a tall tale

Such as…

You cannot turn a Hoe

Into a housewife

Even if your living well

Sounds like something I heard before

I told my elder

She was never faithful

He replied "she's just being herself"

"But I thought I told you bout these hoes"

The Chapters of pain

In my past is a reflection

Of everything they knew

That I dismissed

With a pretentious laugh

Now…

My soul is a dark hole

Where my dreams and nightmares

Are one in the same

And my fears feed my rage

Just to entertain the demons

In this space.

Yet I still manage to get comfortable

And find solace in the pain

So every day I wake

It's like I climbed

Out of that hole

Stronger than before like Bane.

Though my past actions

Has me in a present day

That's not so lavish

At least today

I can tame the addict

So maybe my tomorrow's

Do not seem as tragic.

But then I think

My tomorrows would not

Seem like the same day

If I did not have the habit

Then I remember

An elder saying

With every bag I'm accepting

Not embracing the pain.

Examples of men from yesterday

Becomes foresight into the future

Yes, I'm here to inspire change.

SHE'S BITCH

She's a Bitch

But still I give her all of me

And give even more

Every time I share my weed.

I don't love her like I used to

But I'm not ready to leave

Even though I hate who

She's become

I still give her everything.

Every pretty penny pinched attached

To my hopes and dreams

I sacrifice to satisfy

Her wants and needs.

She's a bitch and never been

Faithful to a King

A queen to many men

Her adoration in the moment

Reflects my greed.

Even though she's a bitch

She tends the soil that feeds

My family tree, that stems from

Poisonous seeds that houses

Medicated leaves on branches

Of cancerous thoughts.

That fuel an addicted drive

And dreams of successful scenes

As my addiction shines and comes

To life under the sunlight.

She's a bitch but she understands

A good man can't be righteous

All of the time.

I RAN OUTTA FUCKS TO GIVE

WHILE LOSSING MY PERSPECTIVE

OF WHAT RIGHT IS

BUT AT LEAST I GET TO FUCK

MY CHICK TONIGHT.

I knew the devil was a lie

When I heard Jesus Walks

And seen a wolf disguised

As the shepherd of the lord.

Using the influence of scripture

To mold the manipulation

And offer us a way to relate

On a path we cannot afford.

Bribing the people

Showing off the blessing he bought

We empty our pockets so he can

Be touched by the hand of GOD.

The Devil is a lie

But the Devil is alive and told me

I need not believe in the beliefs

Of the village way before 2Chainz

Was in Tru Religion fulfilling birthday wishes.

We've seen our heroes

Go from warning us of the dangerous

Of bedding a cave bitch

To being a Captain on a

Financial slave ship.

We have let crooked men explain

What righteous sin is

I'm saying, I see the seeds of evil

In the righteous eyes

That lead the people

In these rappers' lines.

Then I roll up that lethal

And devise a plan with the divine

To save them all

With the use of my third eye

And a Shakespearian mind.

The devil is alive and told me

I would never know heaven until I

Inhaled the flakes of angle wings

The profitable information that came

Was intoxicating and forced me

To seek the GOD in me.

Water will quench their thirst

Alcoholic drinks will make them thirsty

It's codependency for all those

Who don't love me

Wisdom is understanding you position

In that Ponzi scheme.

Yes, the devil is a lie

But my fuel for this greed

Is a narcotic from Christ and I'm addicted

To everything deserving of a King

Power, Influence, appointed accountability

And enough money to speak

Every language fluently.

Using spirituality as the blueprint

I lock in this money scheme

In the hearts of those

Willing to follow his lead

Yes, the Devil is alive

And in cahoots with the

GOD in me.

The Devil is a lie

But the Devil is alive in areas

Where the truth resides

Politicking with Christ

Damn Kanye Why?

PROUD

The original man can never be
A stereotype
We are the indigenous seeds
That binds spirituality to life.

Thus making us the clay that
Molds all personality archetypes
He talks White
Is the perspective of a slaves mind.

My intellectual speech is the
First step I use to rise
And fight the good fight.

So, you can see why
"My Nigga"
Is the connective thread
In the knot that keeps
The noose tied.

How a slave thinks is infectious
To the idle hands of free man
With the ability to affect time.

Colonizers with effective schemes

Have affected how the

Rhythm and message intertwine

Now we are sleep walking

Searching for the method.

Believing the popular truth

Is a placebo we use to

Avoid the friction and feel

The sensation of loosening binds.

If I must be anything more

Then the intellectual properties

My melanin decrees

Just to be proud to be

Then never mind.

I'm still an individual looking

For a righteous path with evil eyes

Struggling to find a decent meal

To eat free from swine

Though I eat with the same filth

To acquire a way to provide.

The duality of life is as intricate

As the feeling of the stated

Double entendre

"I'm putting my emotions into a line"

But the right fist

That accompanies that pain

Gives me a reason to be alive

I'm proud of the man

Our History has made.

ROOTED DEATH

I want to hang myself

From a tree

Because the racist inside my soul

Wants to kill the stereotypes

That knot my cultural ties

Now that's what you call hatred

But I call it drive.

The drugs I can't leave alone

Has snapped the neck of my conscious

In the same fashion good ol boy

Used to do to the indigenous slaves

Walking alone on dirt roads

Hung from a tree.

To make America Great

They are trying to use

The same tactics today, no wonder

Racism is the separation that binds us

Your participation doesn't require

The truth to determine what you believe.

While my culture falls behind

Chasing the ism – they stood pat

And made slavery a privatized system

Forgotten dreams are captured in

The smoke of the swisher sweet

And Turned into wisdom.

I'm an equal opportunity racist

But they still want to see me

With my feet dangling gasping for air

Because my speech spreads hatred

For the one percent equally.

But even if they restrain

My neck to this oak tree

I am well prepared

I'll use my last breath to send

A black fist emoji to inspire those

The revolution lost to the screens

Freedom comes at a price everywhere.

They can get the rope but I'll

Never swallow my pride and choke

On the truth

They got us to put on a black face

While lighting our shade just to

Behave in their perception of black

That is their cultural money move.

Tie em up with the gold ropes

They use to manipulate my kind

And drown them in a sea of blood

Lost in the soil of diamond minds

So, my future seeds can look up

To see me shinning.

My minds a gem and glows

In the darkness

Where men get lost searching for hope

But the echo of my quotes

Is a Clippers Jersey turned inside out

For my folks.

We were Kings and Queens

Before we were slaves and we escaped

Servitude but have not removed

The mental restraints

Hang em' Up.

UNARMED AND GUN DOWNED

If a Black Man is riddled

With 20 bullets in his community

Does it make a sound?

Am I supposed to believe?

Justice will be delivered with

Camera footage and multiple witnesses around

Tell me, what is the proper decorum

For a resolution before the revolution

When the reality is

They want my people

Unarmed and Gun Downed.

I stand here black and proud

As a revolutionary, actively acting

As an intellectual fighter, a future martyr

I know tomorrow isn't promised

If suspicions of criminal intentions

Give them the right to make me a victim

But I clinch my book tighter.

As my palms sweat from the excitement

Of positive knowledge

The original man and women

Are descendants of Gods

It's that realization that helps us

Defy the odds.

Wille lynch knew he no longer

Needed to lynch men

To turn fear into profit

Ignorance turns into dollar signs

In the face of real logic.

Orchestrate the hate manipulate the victims

Industrialize the solution and for decades

You have a culture

To preoccupied to remove the

Restraints of figurative nooses.

I remain unphased by the

Thoughts of sheep

To prepared to lose

Standing here in my hoodie

Ready to die today

For intellectual conquest

And to save the fools.

I put my fist up in a poem

Before I understood the power

Of hope

Hit harder for my people

Then the fist I used for prevention

Who knew?

I found the truth and couldn't see

The use of the church

After I studied Jim Crow.

So, I've seen most preachers

The same way I seen

The pushers in the hood

A colorful negro used

To sale the sheep hope.

Unarmed and Gun Downed

Is the sentence for black folks

Yet they want me on my knees

Seeking repentance

Praying to ghost

As my innocence is slayed

Unarmed and Gun Downed

Like all the forgotten names

Subjected to rage and bad aim

With dreams of doing more

Unarmed and Gun Downed like B. Taylor

Unarmed and Gun Downed for being

Unruly in a store like - Mike Brown

They want me Unarmed and Gun Downed

In the streets are restricted to a compound

Because I dare to speak.

I twist a leaf and get mad twisted

Because my quest for knowledge extends

Further than the reach of organized religion

And for that

They want me Unarmed and Gun Downed

Or serving an economic life sentence

They want us shackled and locked

Admiring money power and respect

The same may Mr. Combs had aspiring artist

When he was jerking the Lox

Schools with more locks than books

Lead to poor education

Now we can't properly articulate

Our rage we burn their shit down

Now it looks like a ghost town

On our blocks

There must be a better way.

With my hands up

I lived the life of

A thousand black men as

The reflection of my watch face

Becomes a shiny knife

And they shoot until their fear

Feels justified

Unarmed and Gun Downed

Though still we rise.

GRAY HAIRED ADOLESCENTS

I've lost sight of time

Forgot my age and remember

I still have dreams.

As I stare at the descending sands

In my rear view I move forward

Manipulating the history

Of my timeline cause things

Are not always what they seem.

When you see a man

In a "Nigga" born to lose

Excel in a rhyme scheme

And bring meaning to emotions

That meant nothing to you

You began to understand success

Is like your first suit

Something you need to grow in to.

I was a drug dealer once

A street walker, a sneaker pimp

And a thief

A loser in the suit of a winner

I was considered a failure

If I didn't overachieve.

My youth returns like the seasons

After a cold winter.

Repeatedly reminding me

There is still time for me to

Complete what I set out to achieve

I am ready to fail

So, I am prepared to live

This is what I believe.

I'll die a thousand emotional deaths

Before I'd admit It's over for me

I still define my present

By my future endeavors

Anticipating I will become

The person I'd thought I'd be

And I am getting closer.

I can't recall a memory

Of when I focused sober

So, I hit the weed and engage

In a reality that

I am running away from

In place, forced to play a game

Where the participants are constantly

Looked over.

The intensity of time

Is based off perception

And the seconds are picking up speed

Though if I stay forever young

You could never say it's over for me.

INTOXICATED MEMORIES

When my weed habit

Was so close to snorting powder

I was ready to stand tall

And fight the power.

To better lead the sheep and cowards

To the clear waters and apple trees

Reserved for royalty

Ready to ride for the family

Until my final hour.

BUT NOW...

My cocaine habit cost

More than a lump sum of dollars

And I'm fighting the power

Of my addiction everyday

Searching for a better me.

Back to Back Swisher Sweets

And a non-fiction book to read

In the clouds overstanding

The laws used to raise and govern kings.

I sniff one, I sniff two, then sniff three

I want to change but it's clear

History is destined to repeat

I'm the result of inspiration

Found in negative speech.

What is left of my soul to save

Has been lost in the catacombs

Of my sober memoires

I remember

When my weed was like cocaine

Today cocaine has weed

Searching for a new identity.

ROLLING WITH THE PUNCHES

A rolled dollar in the shorts

I wore last summer

Is used to gather

Inspiration from my favorite album cover.

The dollar I rolled yesterday

Is a remainder a dollar saved

Is a future tool for better days

Or a contribution to financial waste

When its promised to intoxicate

Though that knowledge

Is worth the mental drain.

The dollar rolled

That I forgot about

Will be the next symbol

I used to illustrate

How I try to get away

From myself but can't seem to escape.

Every dollar paves the way

For me to embrace my bad habits

Like my reflection

It's something I can alter

But the foundation stays the same

The pleasure last forever

But all I can remember is the pain.

For too long I have been

Addicted to the game

Chasing the high and chasing death

Basically, at this point

You can say this is my attempt

To run away from old age.

The last dollar I rolled

Numbs the pain

Now my tomorrows

Feel like yesterday.

ADDICTIVE SUBMISSION
(DEATH BY A THOUSAND CUT'S)

Death by a thousand cuts

Is a slow death, I realized this

As I'm rolling my

Nine Hundred and nineth ninth blunt.

The blunt lit, I'm ready to die

My high has outlived

My potential and I'm

At the end of the line.

Seeing none and every reason why

To see my life intertwine

With what was

Now my future is hunted

By barrowed time.

I've lived a nightmare

In a dream rolling up

Intending to close my eyes

Praying they stay shut.

But, the opportunity in the light

Is intoxicating so I've jumped

In a line to get ahead

Now I'm all the way up

Eyes wide shut.

The mantra of my razors edge, is

Pleasure is found in a thousand cuts

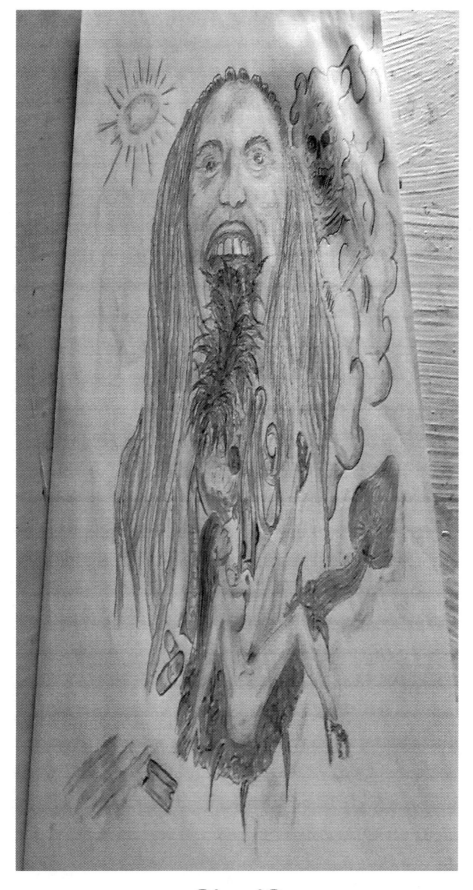

REST IN PEACE SEAN PRICE

Yoooooooo.

I spent a lot of gotdamn time

Writing lines off lines

Banging Sean Price

Working to make these poems

Appeal to niggas that rhyme

But this time, I must be

Outta my gotdamn damn mind

Or channeling the God

At the same time, he is in

The booth with Christ.

Because this penmanship is an

Exquisite event that satin

Would pay to attend

So, as I look the devil

In the eyes holding a spliff

I aim to sooth the hearts

Of men like gospel hymns

I'm like wawp baba lowap

Bop boom bap boom

I swear to the flag

On the moon Ima better fit

If you, working through

Emotions to live

Why would I lie to you?

I bug with words

Smoke a blunt, read a comic,

Watch Sci-fi,

Then role play with my girl

Peace to Allah as I benefit

From the seeds of Mother Earth.

I remain smooth

As the Newport is used

To wipe coce off the card

Dudes want the juice but aint

Strong enough to squeeze fruit

Word is bon.

Ima bona-fide certified good weed roller

Getting high enough to see

The stars with the world

On my shoulders

Ice trays have never been colder

Jesus Price

Heaven got another solider.

WINE FOR THE MOMENT

I want a glass of wine

But I'm too ugly to go outside

I mean I'm cute and all

Even pretty in the right light.

But the emotional stains of the day

Has wrinkled the sleeves

Of my favorite outfit

Now this fabric

Just don't feel right.

I swear a glass of Merlot

Would set the vibe

But my disdain

For the decision made

To parallel popular minds

Is summarized by the

"FUCK YOU" expression on my face.

Word to saving the day

I would love a glass of wine

But their perception of my

Beauty offends me

So, it's best that I don't

Leave the confines of my

Safe space and socialize.

My conscious is

A bottle I just opened up

It needs time to breath.

But Damn

The legs on a cabernet

Are so nice.

But I'm too ugly to indulge

And go outside.

I mean I'm a few numbers

North of a five

And my aura is live

But these turkeys are foul

And will only comply

If you shuck and jive

And that aint me.

Yo, I swear

I want a glass of wine

But the travel seems like

A waste of time

Since my D.D. just arrived

And the impending clouds

Will set me free.

ELEGANT HIGH

I'm not just a stoner smoking

I am an artist cloud surfing

Riding the waves of creativity

Vibing feeling the energy

This glass design is the source

That provides the clouds I ride

Like Guko to discover

The dragon balls of imagination

That will give me the power

To write with the influence

To save lives.

As my mental transformation

On the sheet takes the form

Of an androsphinx

In search of emotional control

This pen becomes the God

And Warden that rehabilitate

The demons in my soul.

My G that scheme should serve

As clever imagery into

The depths of the smoke

Is it ironic the high is deep?

My folks say

"You can only get so high"

I reply

"I've never seen that ceiling"

The same way I never seen

A tear in a dove eye

Even when the high reached heights

To use the wings of angels

For spiritual healing.

No matter the physical or emotional pain

I use the euphoric touch

Of Mary Jane

To do away with that feeling.

RANDOM

Have you ever seen Belly?

Have you ever seen Belly on weed?

Man, that movie is best

When your high.

I use good green

To make reality seem like real life

Though I'm a hippie at heart

And love to extend the vibes

Don't come around me scavenging

Unless you got five.

M.V.P. (MOST VALUABLE POET)

I remember the days when I had to

Sleep on park benches

Now the park is the stage

For my soapbox

Where I express my adolescent rage

As experience and wisdom

But who's listening.

When every lame with a chain

Is in a lane claiming

King trying to flex

With a motive to leave an impression

Not to impress with a message

The result is a hopeless reflection

Of the toxicity

We used to define ourselves

While the legend of the prowess

Of my right hand

Grows in poor and rich homes

Alike like a chia pet.

In my mind I keep

Twenty-Six letters in an infinite amount

Of combinations at my disposal

Like Allah breath

That's why I propose

My nouns and Verbs in

Immaculate pros are a Godsend

Anywhere I can find a pen

I can call my home

So, the world is my castle

Where I polish the crown

My head holds

They say a picture

Is worth a thousand words

Making every photo with a black fist up

A thousand signatures from

The past and present petitioning for hope

Though I say nothing

To say everything and continue to vote

I ask how we are supposed to grow

When the soil is contaminated

With pesticides of ignorance

The harvest is bountiful but its intent

Is to stunt intellectual growth

Most valuable poet

After the murder her wrote

Ink bleeds out of control

Like a wrist after a suicide attempt

Telling a story on scattered pages

Like the blood splatter on the floor

Leaving directions to God truth

In every line I wrote.

SOLD MY SOUL

I sold my soul to the devil

And the price was cheap

I forsake him and sacrifice my needs

To satisfy my wants

With a big booty freak.

I signed the contract in blood

To define the purity of my beliefs

That one plus one is two

But I can turn one into three.

I can…

Find a reality in a dream

Euphoria in seeds

Live the life of a king

Without a dollar in my jeans.

The cost of happiness

Is priceless to me and since

Love doesn't cost a thing

Love doesn't' hold a pennies weight

To a G.

Some say I've lost it

But all I can offer is

The best of me since I'm

The reality of what the cost is

I sold my soul to the devil

And signed the contract with

The excess from a rolled dollar bill

The euphoria that followed was

Fictional but the cost was real

Though I live a comfortable life

To some the rewards will never

Exceed the value of the deal.

The reflection of my future dissipates

Like my precious minerals and crystals

At the end of my razor blade

And I don't know how to feel.

I sold my soul to the devil

With an option to restructure the deal

For the second half

Of my life if I provide a seed

To continue his legacy of manipulating

Man's will.

The best of me

Reflected my pencil

Now the sharpness of my

Lead is a digital memory

I share with the people

Separate and lethal posing a threat

To those who pose as my equal.

THEY COME BIGGER NOW

Things aren't the way

They used to be

When I was a child

First the Roc breaks up

Then Lil Kim "Mike Jack" her face up

And white boys can say nigga now.

But how can I be

Surprised by the changes

When I look around because

They didn't then but

White women come with fatter asses now.

The feeling isn't what it once was

I could feel the spirit walking

Among us proud with her fist up.

But a New World Order has

Designed the times

Actors posing as politicians with celebrity wives

Private eyes manipulating our social interest

The screens have made us slaves

To the bottom line.

Though how can I be surprised

At how things ended up

When all I see is white woman

In leggings with bigger butts.

What you feel isn't real

And the real

Have been compromised for ones

Though I'm not surprised

When we celebrate are women

Getting ass shots as if

What God gave them isn't good enough.

But white women come with

Fatter asses now

So, more is never enough

Now I do two lines

Off her back side

Instead of a couple bumps.

These gray hairs are a testament

To the things I used to love

Everything around me is changing

Except the quality of my drugs.

I wonder when Bill Clinton

Was getting special attention

If he knew his misses could

Make a run at presidency

When white women

Came with bigger butts.

CHAOS IN MY MIND

I sit in the center of

The chaos in my mind

Taunted by the faces

Of my emotions.

I try to control them

But their emotional patterns

Change at a moment's notice

And none of them feel like mine.

I look closer and I am taking back

By their expression of disappointment

It is clear my reflection

Been living a lie.

Walking a line in a loop

Repeating the patterns, I used

To find happiness the day

After my dreams died.

As the chaos ensues

The faces stay still

While time moves

I'm haunted by the minutes

As the seconds keep passing me by.

Their expression changes

And I'm subsumed by their

Anger and rage the hopelessness and pain.

Hence why in my current state

I am faking it everyday

In hopes that we make it

The honesty in that reflection

Is a prelude to the looming loneliness.

These gray hairs are proof

That destiny can be mistaken

It is a whirlwind in my mind

And I'm at the mercy of my faces.

FADED INTELLECTUAL

I am a faded intellectual

My concept flourish in the contexts

As the swisher blows

I freak the alphabet

Then have mind sex

When the dollars rolled.

When the liquor pours

I'll drown a lame duck in metaphors

The same way I do my advisories

With strategic strategies of war

Without remorse.

On my conquest addressing the struggle

Understanding the simplicity

They attempt to make complex

In my zone walking alone

As a faded intellectual.

Intelligently intoxicated breaking down

The alphabet meticulously

To retrieve prophetic statements

Of what life means

That was lost by those translating

The Basic Instructions Before Leaving Earth.

By those who looked to seize

The future by manipulating history first

A faded intellectual

With a purpose and a dream

A sedated individual sainted inspiring change

In crisp jeans, a designer tee and Fila

Walking the streets protecting the jewels

In my notebook like

The book of Eli.

I aim to present to you

My passion not participate

In a fools game

Those participants are banal

And would gladly suck

On the penal for fame

Or remain complacent

With the pressure of failure

In their face.

I aggressively press the status quo

Hoping to replace the economic restraints

Design to help us fade to black

But I stay faded

Manipulating the current structure

Ready to fight back

As a faded intellectual.

Printed in the United States
By Bookmasters